GLUCOSE REVOLUTION COOKBOOK

Inspired By Jessie Inchauspe's Revolutionary Teachings

80 Recipes for Balancing and Maintaining Healthy Blood Sugar Levels that anyone can cook

Loveth Iwinosa

Copyright

PREFERENCE

The Art of Eating for Glucose Balance

Forget crash diets, calorie counting, and food restrictions—this cookbook isn't about telling you what to eat. Instead, it's about something far more powerful: how you eat.

The truth is, the way we eat has an enormous impact on our blood sugar levels, energy, and overall health. The order in which we eat our food, the way we combine ingredients, and even how we start our meals can mean the difference between steady energy or an afternoon slump, between feeling satisfied or battling cravings all day long.

We're here to take the guesswork out of glucose balance. By making small, simple changes in how you structure your meals—without cutting out your favorite foods—you can experience:

✅ Fewer energy crashes and sugar cravings
✅ Improved metabolism and weight regulation
✅ More stable moods and sharper focus
✅ Better long-term health

In this cookbook, you'll discover delicious, practical recipes designed to help you apply these principles effortlessly. Whether it's "fiber first," pairing carbs with protein and healthy fats, or knowing how to enjoy sweets without the sugar spike, each recipe is crafted to support your glucose stability while keeping your meals flavorful and satisfying.

Are you ready to eat smarter, feel better, and enjoy food in a whole new way? Let's dive in.

ABOUT THE AUTHOR

Loveth Iwinosa is a passionate culinary expert and food enthusiast who loves creating memorable meals that unite people. With years of experience in both professional kitchens and home cooking, Loveth has mastered the art of blending simplicity with creativity, making delicious recipes accessible to everyone.

A self-taught chef turned cookbook author, Loveth's journey began with experimenting in her grandmother's kitchen, where she learned the value of fresh ingredients and soulful cooking. Over the years, her dedication to the culinary arts has earned her recognition for crafting recipes that are not only flavorful but also practical for busy lifestyles.

When she's not in the kitchen, Loveth enjoys exploring global cuisines, seeking inspiration for new dishes, and sharing her culinary adventures with a growing community of food lovers. Through this cookbook, she aims to inspire readers to embrace the joy of cooking, one recipe at a time.

Loveth Iwinosa lives by the motto, "Great meals start with passion and end with satisfaction." Whether you're a seasoned cook or a kitchen newbie, her approachable style and flavorful recipes promise to transform everyday cooking into an extraordinary experience.

TABLE OF CONTENTS

INTRODUCTION
The Power of Eating Smart

Most diets focus on what to eat. They hand you a list of "good" and "bad" foods, tell you to cut carbs or avoid sugar, and leave you feeling restricted, frustrated, and stuck in an endless cycle of deprivation and cravings.

This cookbook is different.

Here, we focus on how to eat—because the way you eat has a more powerful effect on your glucose levels than you might think. You don't have to give up your favorite foods or live off salads to maintain steady energy and avoid glucose spikes. Instead, you just need to learn a few simple hacks that will change how your body processes what you eat.

When we eat the right way—by prioritizing fiber, following the best food order, and pairing our meals properly—we can enjoy the foods we love without the blood sugar rollercoaster. And when our glucose levels are steady, we experience:

✅ More energy—no more afternoon crashes or post-meal sluggishness

✅ Fewer cravings—stabilizing blood sugar reduces hunger swings

✅ Better metabolism—balanced glucose helps the body burn fat efficiently

✅ Improved focus and mood—goodbye brain fog, hello clarity

✅ Sustainable health—protecting against diabetes, inflammation, and aging

This cookbook is your guide to making these simple yet transformative changes.

What You'll Learn in This Cookbook

Each chapter is designed to help you apply the principles of glucose balance in a way that's practical, delicious, and easy to follow:

🥗 Chapter 1: Fiber First – The Power of Preloading
 Before diving into your meal, eating fiber-rich foods first slows glucose absorption and prevents big sugar spikes. You'll find fiber-packed starters that set you up for balanced meals.

🥑 Chapter 2: The Right Food Order – Controlling Sugar Spikes
 Did you know eating your carbs last can reduce glucose spikes by up to 75%? This chapter shows you how to structure your meals in the most glucose-friendly way.

🍳 Chapter 3: Pairing Carbs with Protein & Fat
 Not all carbs are the enemy—but eating them alone can wreak havoc on blood sugar. Here, you'll learn how to enjoy carbs by pairing them with protein and healthy fats.

🍫 Chapter 4: Smart Sugar Hacks – Enjoying Sweets Without the Crash
 Love desserts? So do we! This chapter teaches you how to enjoy sweet treats without the sugar rollercoaster, so you can indulge guilt-free.

☕ Chapter 5: Drinks & Their Impact on Blood Sugar
 What you drink is just as important as what you eat. We'll explore which beverages spike glucose and which ones stabilize it, plus blood sugar-friendly drink recipes.

🥜 Chapter 6: Blood Sugar-Friendly Snacks & Meal Prep
 Glucose-friendly eating isn't just about main meals—it's also about smart snacking and meal prep. This chapter gives you quick, easy, and portable ideas to stay on track.
A New Way to Eat, A Better Way to Live

Balancing your glucose doesn't mean giving up your favorite foods. It means eating them in a way that supports your body, fuels your energy, and keeps you feeling amazing. This cookbook is here to show you how simple, enjoyable, and effective it can be.
Let's get started!

Chapter 1
Fiber First – The Power of Preloading

Fiber is your secret weapon for controlling glucose spikes. When you eat fiber before other foods, it acts like a protective shield, slowing down the absorption of sugar into your bloodstream. This prevents sudden spikes and crashes, keeping your energy and cravings in check.

Eating fiber first—from leafy greens, vegetables, legumes, or seeds—forms a natural barrier in your digestive system, reducing how quickly glucose enters your bloodstream. The result? A steadier glucose curve, improved digestion, and better overall metabolic health.

In this chapter, you'll find delicious, fiber-rich recipes designed to be eaten before your main meals. From crisp salads to nutrient-packed veggie bowls, these recipes will help you master the "fiber first" principle effortlessly.

FIBER FIRST

RECIPES

WARM LENTIL & SPINACH SALAD

Prep Time : 5 Min

Cook Time : 20 Min

Ingredients:

- 1 cup cooked lentils
- 2 cups fresh spinach
- ½ cup cherry tomatoes, halved
- ¼ red onion, thinly sliced
- 1 tbsp olive oil
- 1 tbsp balsamic vinegar
- ½ tsp salt
- ½ tsp black pepper

Instructions:

- Heat olive oil in a pan over medium heat.
- Add red onion and cook for 2 minutes until softened.
- Add cooked lentils and cherry tomatoes, sauté for 3-4 minutes.
- Toss in fresh spinach, stir for 1 minute until slightly wilted.
- Remove from heat, drizzle with balsamic vinegar, and season with salt and pepper.
- Serve warm, optionally topped with feta cheese or pumpkin seeds.

Toppings: Crumbled feta, pumpkin seeds, or a drizzle of tahini

CRUNCHY CABBAGE SLAW WITH SESAME DRESSING

Prep Time : 5 Min

Cook Time : 15 Min

Ingredients:

- 2 cups shredded cabbage (red or green)
- 1 small carrot, shredded
- ½ cup chopped cilantro
- 1 tbsp sesame seeds
- 1 tbsp olive oil
- 1 tbsp rice vinegar
- 1 tsp sesame oil
- 1 tsp soy sauce or tamari
- ½ tsp honey (optional)

Instructions:

- In a large bowl, combine shredded cabbage, carrot, and cilantro.
- In a small bowl, whisk together olive oil, rice vinegar, sesame oil, soy sauce, and honey.
- Pour the dressing over the slaw and toss to coat.
- Sprinkle with sesame seeds and serve fresh.

Toppings: Crushed peanuts, sliced almonds, or extra sesame seeds

ROASTED CAULIFLOWER & CHICKPEA BOWL

Prep Time : 10 Min

Cook Time : 30 Min

Ingredients:

- 1 small head of cauliflower, cut into florets
- 1 cup canned chickpeas, drained and rinsed
- 1 tbsp olive oil
- ½ tsp cumin
- ½ tsp smoked paprika
- ½ tsp salt
- ½ tsp black pepper

Instructions:

- Preheat oven to 400°F (200°C).
- Toss cauliflower and chickpeas with olive oil, cumin, paprika, salt, and pepper.
- Spread on a baking sheet and roast for 25 minutes, stirring halfway through.
- Serve warm with a squeeze of lemon juice.

Toppings: Greek yogurt, pomegranate seeds, or tahini drizzle

FIBER-RICH GREEN SMOOTHIE

Prep Time : 1 Min

Cook Time : 5 Min

Ingredients:

- 1 cup spinach
- ½ avocado
- ½ cup cucumber, chopped
- 1 tbsp chia seeds
- 1 tbsp flaxseeds
- 1 cup unsweetened almond milk
- ½ lemon, juiced

Instructions:

- Blend all ingredients until smooth.
- Pour into a glass and enjoy immediately.

Toppings: Hemp seeds, shredded coconut, or a sprinkle of cinnamon

FLAX & CHIA CRACKERS WITH HUMMUS

Prep Time : 15 Min

Cook Time : 40 Min

Ingredients:

- ½ cup ground flaxseeds
- ¼ cup chia seeds
- ½ cup water
- ½ tsp garlic powder
- ½ tsp salt
- ½ tsp black pepper

Instructions:

- Preheat oven to 325°F (165°C).
- Mix all ingredients in a bowl and let sit for 10 minutes until thick.
- Spread the mixture thinly on a parchment-lined baking sheet.
- Bake for 30 minutes or until crisp.
- Break into pieces and serve with hummus.

Toppings: Sprinkle with sesame seeds or cracked black pepper

WARM QUINOA & ROASTED VEGGIE BOWL

Prep Time : 10 Min

Cook Time : 35 Min

Ingredients:

- 1 cup cooked quinoa
- ½ cup roasted zucchini, sliced
- ½ cup roasted bell peppers, chopped
- ½ cup roasted eggplant, diced
- 1 tbsp olive oil
- ½ tsp dried oregano
- ½ tsp salt
- ½ tsp black pepper

Instructions:

- Preheat oven to 400°F (200°C).
- Toss zucchini, bell peppers, and eggplant with olive oil, oregano, salt, and pepper.
- Spread on a baking sheet and roast for 25 minutes, stirring halfway through.
- Mix with cooked quinoa and serve warm.

Toppings: Feta cheese, toasted pine nuts, or fresh parsley

BERRY & ALMOND YOGURT BOWL

Prep Time : 1 Min

Cook Time : 5 Min

Ingredients:

- ½ cup Greek yogurt (unsweetened)
- ¼ cup mixed berries (blueberries, raspberries, strawberries)
- 1 tbsp chia seeds
- 1 tbsp slivered almonds
- ½ tsp cinnamon

Instructions:

- In a bowl, mix Greek yogurt with cinnamon.
- Top with berries, chia seeds, and almonds.
- Serve fresh.

Toppings: Strawberry, mint leaves, berries, or a drizzle of almond butter

CHIA SEED PUDDING WITH BERRIES

Prep Time : 1 Min

Cook Time : 5 Min

Ingredients:

- ¼ cup chia seeds
- 1 cup unsweetened almond milk (or any plant-based milk)
- ½ tsp vanilla extract
- ½ tsp cinnamon (optional)
- 1 tbsp maple syrup or honey (optional)
- ½ cup mixed berries (strawberries, blueberries, raspberries)

Instructions:

- In a bowl or jar, mix chia seeds, almond milk, vanilla extract, and cinnamon. Stir well to combine.
- Let it sit for 5 minutes, then stir again to prevent clumping.
- Cover and refrigerate for at least 2 hours or overnight until thick and pudding-like.
- Before serving, top with fresh berries and enjoy!

Toppings: Strawberry, berries, or a drizzle of nut butter

AVOCADO & FLAXSEED SALAD

Prep Time : 1 Min

Cook Time : 5 Min

Ingredients:

- 1 ripe avocado, diced
- 2 cups mixed greens (spinach, arugula, or kale)
- ½ cucumber, sliced
- ¼ cup cherry tomatoes, halved
- 1 tbsp ground flaxseeds
- 1 tbsp olive oil
- 1 tbsp lemon juice
- ½ tsp salt
- ½ tsp black pepper
- 1 boiled egg

Instructions:

- In a large bowl, combine mixed greens, cucumber, cherry tomatoes, and diced avocado.
- Sprinkle with ground flaxseeds.
- In a small bowl, whisk together olive oil, lemon juice, salt, and pepper.
- Drizzle dressing over the salad, toss gently, and serve immediately.

Toppings: Crushed walnuts, hemp seeds, or feta cheese

ROASTED BRUSSELS SPROUTS WITH LEMON TAHINI

Prep Time : 1 Min

Cook Time : 5 Min

Ingredients:

- 2 cups Brussels sprouts, trimmed and halved
- 1 tbsp olive oil
- ½ tsp salt
- ½ tsp black pepper

For the Lemon Tahini Sauce:

- 2 tbsp tahini
- 1 tbsp lemon juice
- 1 clove garlic, minced
- 1 tbsp warm water (to thin)
- ½ tsp maple syrup or honey (optional)

Instructions:

- Preheat oven to 400°F (200°C).
- Toss Brussels sprouts with olive oil, salt, and pepper.
- Spread on a baking sheet in a single layer and roast for 25 minutes, flipping halfway through.
- While roasting, whisk together tahini, lemon juice, garlic, warm water, and maple syrup in a small bowl. Adjust consistency if needed.
- Drizzle the lemon tahini sauce over the roasted Brussels sprouts before serving.

Toppings: Toasted sesame seeds, crushed almonds, or chili flakes

Chapter 2
The Right Food Order – Controlling Sugar Spikes

Most people don't think about the order in which they eat their food—but science shows that meal sequencing plays a crucial role in glucose control. How you structure your meals can significantly impact how your body processes sugar, influencing energy levels, hunger, and even fat storage.

Why Food Order Matters

When you eat carbohydrates first—such as bread, rice, or pasta—glucose floods into your bloodstream quickly, leading to a sharp spike in blood sugar. This spike is often followed by a crash, triggering cravings, fatigue, and hunger shortly after. However, following the right food sequence can slow down glucose absorption and keep your energy stable throughout the day.

The Ideal Meal Sequence for Glucose Control

To balance blood sugar and reduce spikes, follow this simple four-step eating order:

1 Start with Fiber – Eating fiber first creates a gel-like layer in the gut, slowing down glucose absorption. This prevents sugar spikes and keeps you fuller for longer. (Examples: leafy greens, vegetables, beans, chia seeds, flaxseeds)

2 Eat Protein & Healthy Fats Next – Protein and fat further slow digestion and help regulate the release of glucose into the bloodstream. They also prevent insulin surges, which helps with weight management. (Examples: eggs, fish, meat, nuts, avocado, olive oil)

3 Have Carbohydrates Last – When carbs are eaten after fiber, protein, and fats, their impact on blood sugar is significantly reduced. Instead of causing a glucose spike, they enter the bloodstream at a slower rate. (Examples: rice, potatoes, bread, pasta, fruit)

4 Save Sugary Foods for the End – If you're having dessert, eat it after a balanced meal rather than on an empty stomach. This minimizes its effect on blood sugar. (Examples: chocolate, pastries, fruit juices, candies)

How This Works in Real Life

Let's take a common meal—grilled chicken with rice and a side of vegetables. Here's how to eat it strategically:

✔ Start with the veggies (fiber)
✔ Eat the chicken (protein and fat)
✔ Finish with the rice (carbohydrates)

By making this simple change, you can reduce glucose spikes by up to 75%, leading to more stable energy, fewer cravings, and better metabolic health.

Glucose-Friendly Recipes to Follow the Right Order

This chapter includes recipes that naturally follow the best food sequencing, such as:

🥗 Fiber First Starters: Warm Lentil & Spinach Salad, Crunchy Cabbage Slaw

🍗 Protein & Fat Mains: Avocado & Flaxseed Salad, Roasted Brussels Sprouts with Lemon Tahini

🥣 Balanced Carbohydrate Dishes: Quinoa & Roasted Veggie Bowl

By applying this simple method, you can enjoy your favorite foods while maintaining steady glucose levels. Small tweaks, big impact—your body will thank you!

THE RIGHT FOOD ORDER

RECIPES

SPINACH & AVOCADO SCRAMBLE

Prep Time : 3 Min

Cook Time : 10 Min

Ingredients:

- 2 eggs
- 1 tbsp olive oil
- ½ avocado, sliced
- 1 cup fresh spinach
- ¼ tsp salt
- ¼ tsp black pepper

Instructions:

- Heat olive oil in a pan over medium heat.
- Add spinach and sauté for 1-2 minutes until wilted.
- Crack eggs into the pan and scramble gently.
- Season with salt and pepper, then remove from heat.
- Serve with sliced avocado.

Toppings: Feta cheese, red pepper flakes, or a drizzle of tahini

BROCCOLI & CHICKPEA STIR-FRY

Prep Time : 5 Min

Cook Time : 15 Min

Ingredients:

- 1 cup broccoli florets
- ½ cup canned chickpeas, drained
- 1 tbsp olive oil
- 1 clove garlic, minced
- 1 tsp soy sauce or tamari

Instructions:

- Heat olive oil in a pan over medium heat.
- Add garlic and sauté for 30 seconds.
- Add broccoli and chickpeas, cooking for 5-7 minutes until tender.
- Stir in soy sauce and cook for 1 more minute.

Toppings: Sesame seeds, crushed peanuts, or chili flakes

GARLIC BUTTER SHRIMP WITH SAUTÉED KALE

Prep Time : 5 Min

Cook Time : 15 Min

Ingredients:

- ½ lb shrimp, peeled and deveined
- 2 cups kale, chopped
- 1 tbsp butter or ghee
- 1 clove garlic, minced
- ½ tsp salt

Instructions:

- Heat butter in a pan over medium heat.
- Add garlic and shrimp, cooking for 2-3 minutes per side.
- Remove shrimp and add kale to the pan, cooking until wilted.
- Serve shrimp over kale.

Toppings: Lemon zest, grated Parmesan, or a drizzle of olive oil

ZUCCHINI NOODLES WITH PESTO & GRILLED CHICKEN

Prep Time : 5 Min

Cook Time : 20 Min

Ingredients:

- 2 medium zucchinis, spiralized
- 1 grilled chicken breast, sliced
- 2 tbsp pesto
- 1 tbsp olive oil
- ½ tsp salt

Instructions:

- Heat olive oil in a pan over medium heat.
- Add zucchini noodles and sauté for 2 minutes.
- Stir in pesto and cook for another minute.
- Top with sliced grilled chicken and serve.

Toppings: Pine nuts, cherry tomatoes, or grated Parmesan

SALMON WITH ROASTED BRUSSELS SPROUTS

Prep Time : 5 Min

Cook Time : 25 Min

Ingredients:

- 1 salmon fillet
- 1 cup Brussels sprouts, halved
- 1 tbsp olive oil
- ½ tsp salt
- ½ tsp black pepper

Instructions:

- Preheat oven to 400°F (200°C).
- Toss Brussels sprouts with olive oil, salt, and pepper, then roast for 20 minutes.
- In a pan, sear the salmon for 4 minutes per side.
- Serve with roasted Brussels sprouts.

Toppings: Lemon wedges, fresh dill, or a drizzle of balsamic glaze

GREEK YOGURT & WALNUT BOWL

Prep Time : 1 Min
Cook Time : 5 Min

Ingredients:

- ½ cup Greek yogurt
- 2 tbsp walnuts, chopped
- 1 tbsp chia seeds
- ½ tsp cinnamon

Instructions:

- In a bowl, mix Greek yogurt with cinnamon.
- Top with walnuts and chia seeds.

Toppings: Hemp seeds, shredded coconut, or fresh berries

EGGPLANT & CHICKPEA STEW

Prep Time : 5 Min

Cook Time : 30 Min

Ingredients:

- 1 medium eggplant, diced
- ½ cup canned chickpeas, drained
- 1 tbsp olive oil
- 1 clove garlic, minced
- ½ cup diced tomatoes

Instructions:

- Heat olive oil in a pan over medium heat.
- Add garlic and eggplant, sauté for 5 minutes.
- Stir in chickpeas and tomatoes, then simmer for 20 minutes.

Toppings: Fresh parsley, feta cheese, or tahini drizzle

ROASTED CAULIFLOWER & LENTIL BOWL

Prep Time : 5 Min

Cook Time : 30 Min

Ingredients:

- 1 cup cooked lentils
- 1 small cauliflower, cut into florets
- 1 tbsp olive oil
- ½ tsp cumin

Instructions:

- Preheat oven to 400°F (200°C).
- Toss cauliflower with olive oil and cumin, then roast for 25 minutes.
- Mix with lentils and serve.

Toppings: Pomegranate seeds, fresh herbs, or a squeeze of lemon

CABBAGE & AVOCADO WRAPS

Prep Time : 2 Min

Cook Time : 10 Min

Ingredients:

- 2 large cabbage leaves
- ½ avocado, mashed
- ¼ cup shredded chicken
- 1 tbsp hummus

Instructions:

- Spread mashed avocado on cabbage leaves.
- Top with shredded chicken and hummus.
- Roll up and serve.

Toppings: Crushed nuts, sesame seeds, or red pepper flakes

CAULIFLOWER RICE & GRILLED TOFU BOWL

Prep Time : 5 Min

Cook Time : 20 Min

Ingredients:

- 1 cup cauliflower rice
- ½ cup grilled tofu, cubed
- 1 tbsp olive oil
- ½ tsp turmeric

Instructions:

- Heat olive oil in a pan over medium heat.
- Add cauliflower rice and turmeric, cooking for 5 minutes.
- Top with grilled tofu and serve.

Toppings: Cilantro, sesame seeds, or a drizzle of tahini

MISO SOUP WITH TOFU & GREENS

Prep Time : 5 Min

Cook Time : 15 Min

Ingredients:

- 2 cups vegetable broth
- 1 tbsp miso paste
- ½ cup tofu, cubed
- 1 cup bok choy

Instructions:

- Heat broth in a pot over medium heat.
- Stir in miso paste until dissolved.
- Add tofu and bok choy, simmering for 5 minutes.

Toppings: Green onions, sesame seeds, or seaweed

CHICKPEA & SPINACH CURRY

Prep Time : 10 Min

Cook Time : 30 Min

Ingredients:

- 1 cup canned chickpeas, drained
- 2 cups spinach
- 1 tbsp olive oil
- 1 clove garlic, minced
- ½ tsp turmeric

Instructions:

- Heat olive oil in a pan over medium heat.
- Add garlic and chickpeas, cooking for 5 minutes.
- Stir in spinach and turmeric, cooking for 3 minutes.

Toppings: Yogurt, chopped cilantro, or red pepper flakes

Chapter 3:
Pairing Carbs with Protein & Fat - The Science Behind Carb Combinations

Carbohydrates have long been viewed as the main culprit behind glucose spikes. However, the key to better blood sugar control isn't eliminating carbs—it's how you pair them. When carbohydrates are eaten alone, they rapidly break down into glucose, causing a sharp spike in blood sugar. But when paired with protein and fat, digestion slows down, reducing the impact on glucose levels and keeping energy stable for longer.

The Science Behind Carb Pairing

Carbohydrates are broken down into glucose in the digestive system, providing energy for the body. But not all carbs behave the same way. The glycemic impact of a meal depends not just on the carb itself but also on what it's eaten with.

When protein and fat are included in the meal, they:

✅ Slow down digestion – Preventing rapid glucose absorption

✅ Reduce the glucose peak – Creating a steadier blood sugar response

✅ Increase satiety – Keeping you full longer and preventing energy crashes

This is because protein stimulates the release of glucagon, a hormone that counterbalances insulin, while fat delays gastric emptying, meaning carbs enter the bloodstream more gradually.

Practical Application: The Right Food Combinations

By strategically pairing carbs with protein and fat, you can enjoy your favorite carbohydrate-rich foods without extreme blood sugar fluctuations. Here's how:

✅ Pair Whole-Grain Bread with Avocado & Egg

- Instead of plain toast (carbs alone), spread avocado (fat) and top it with a poached egg (protein) for a balanced meal.

✅ Combine Rice with Lentils & Ghee

- White or brown rice alone can cause a glucose spike. Adding lentils (protein & fiber) and a drizzle of ghee or olive oil (fat) slows digestion and stabilizes blood sugar.

✅ Enjoy Pasta with Chicken & Pesto

- Plain pasta can lead to a spike, but pairing it with grilled chicken (protein) and pesto (healthy fats from olive oil & nuts) makes it a more glucose-friendly meal.

✅ Eat Fruits with Nut Butter

- Instead of eating an apple alone, pair it with almond butter for a better blood sugar response. The protein and fat in the nut butter balance out the fruit's natural sugars.

✅ Snack on Dark Chocolate with Nuts

- Instead of sugary chocolate alone, choose dark chocolate (lower sugar, high in antioxidants) and pair it with walnuts or almonds (healthy fat & protein) for a more stable energy release.

By adopting these simple food pairing strategies, you can still enjoy carbohydrates while keeping blood sugar steady, avoiding energy crashes, and improving overall metabolic health.

PAIRING CARBS WITH PROTEIN & FAT

RECIPES

SWEET POTATO & AVOCADO EGG BOWL

Prep Time : 5 Min

Cook Time : 20 Min

Ingredients:

- 1 medium sweet potato, diced
- 1 tbsp olive oil
- 1 boiled egg, sliced
- ½ avocado, mashed
- ½ tsp salt
- ¼ tsp black pepper

Instructions:

- Preheat oven to 400°F (200°C). Toss sweet potatoes with olive oil, salt, and pepper.
- Roast for 15 minutes until soft.
- Serve with sliced egg and mashed avocado.

Toppings: Fresh tomato, chili flakes, sesame seeds, or feta cheese

WHOLE-GRAIN TOAST WITH SALMON & CREAM CHEESE

Prep Time : 3 Min

Cook Time : 10 Min

Ingredients:

- 1 slice whole-grain bread
- 2 tbsp cream cheese
- 2 oz smoked salmon
- ½ tsp lemon zest

Instructions:

- Toast the bread.
- Spread cream cheese over it.
- Top with smoked salmon and lemon zest.

Toppings: Capers, dill, or black pepper

QUINOA & BLACK BEAN BOWL WITH GUACAMOLE

Prep Time : 5 Min

Cook Time : 25 Min

Ingredients:

- ½ cup cooked quinoa
- ½ cup black beans, drained
- 1 tbsp olive oil
- ½ avocado, mashed
- ½ tsp cumin

Instructions:

- Mix quinoa, black beans, olive oil, and cumin.
- Serve topped with mashed avocado.

Toppings: Chopped cilantro, lime juice, or feta cheese

GREEK YOGURT & OATS WITH WALNUTS

Prep Time : 1 Min

Cook Time : 5 Min

Ingredients:

- ½ cup unsweetened Greek yogurt
- ¼ cup rolled oats
- 2 tbsp walnuts, chopped
- ½ tsp cinnamon

Instructions:

- In a bowl, mix Greek yogurt with oats.
- Sprinkle with walnuts and cinnamon.

Toppings: Chopped cilantro, lime juice, or feta cheese

BROWN RICE & LENTIL STIR-FRY WITH TAHINI

Prep Time : 10 Min

Cook Time : 30 Min

Ingredients:

- ½ cup cooked brown rice
- ½ cup cooked lentils
- 1 tbsp tahini
- ½ tsp garlic powder

Instructions:

- Stir-fry brown rice and lentils for 5 minutes.
- Drizzle with tahini and serve

Toppings: Chopped cilantro, lime juice, or feta cheese

AKED OATMEAL WITH ALMOND BUTTER

Prep Time : 10 Min

Cook Time : 30 Min

Ingredients:

- ½ cup rolled oats
- 1 tbsp almond butter
- ½ tsp vanilla extract
- ½ cup unsweetened almond milk

Instructions:

- Preheat oven to 375°F (190°C).
- Mix oats, almond butter, vanilla, and almond milk.
- Bake for 20-25 minutes.

Toppings: Sliced almonds, dark chocolate chips, or chia seeds

CHICKPEA & SPINACH WRAP WITH HUMMUS

Prep Time : 2 Min

Cook Time : 10 Min

Ingredients:

- 1 whole-grain wrap
- ½ cup canned chickpeas, mashed
- ¼ cup spinach, chopped
- 2 tbsp hummus

Instructions:

- Spread hummus over the wrap.
- Add mashed chickpeas and spinach.
- Roll up and serve.

Toppings: Cucumber slices, sunflower seeds, or tahini drizzle

BROWN RICE & GRILLED CHICKEN WITH AVOCADO SALSA

Prep Time : 10 Min

Cook Time : 30 Min

Ingredients:

- ½ cup cooked brown rice
- 1 grilled chicken breast, sliced
- ½ avocado, diced
- ½ cup cherry tomatoes, halved
- 1 tbsp lime juice

Instructions:

- Mix avocado, tomatoes, and lime juice.
- Serve over brown rice with grilled chicken.

Toppings: Cilantro, crumbled feta, or red pepper flakes

WHOLE-GRAIN PASTA WITH PESTO & GRILLED SALMON

Prep Time : 5 Min

Cook Time : 25 Min

Ingredients:

- 1 cup whole-grain pasta
- 1 salmon fillet
- 2 tbsp pesto
- 1 tbsp olive oil

Instructions:

- Cook pasta according to package instructions.
- Grill salmon for 5 minutes per side.
- Toss pasta with pesto and top with salmon.

Toppings: Pine nuts, grated Parmesan, or lemon zest

APPLE & ALMOND BUTTER SNACK

Prep Time : 1 Min
Cook Time : 5 Min

Ingredients:

- 1 apple, sliced
- 1 tbsp almond butter

Instructions:

- Spread almond butter over apple slices.

Toppings: Cinnamon, crushed walnuts, or coconut flakes

COTTAGE CHEESE & BERRIES BOWL WITH FLAXSEEDS

Prep Time : 1 Min

Cook Time : 5 Min

Ingredients:

- ½ cup cottage cheese
- ¼ cup mixed berries
- 1 tbsp ground flaxseeds

Instructions:

- Mix cottage cheese with berries.
- Sprinkle with flaxseeds.

Toppings: Chia seeds, shredded coconut, or honey drizzle

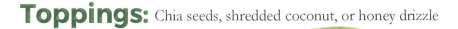

LENTIL SOUP WITH WHOLE-GRAIN CRACKERS

Prep Time : 10 Min

Cook Time : 35 Min

Ingredients:

- 1 cup cooked lentils
- 2 cups vegetable broth
- 1 tbsp olive oil
- ½ tsp cumin
- ½ tsp garlic powder
- 4 whole-grain crackers

Instructions:

- Heat olive oil in a pot.
- Add lentils, broth, cumin, and garlic powder. Simmer for 30 minutes.
- Serve with whole-grain crackers.

Toppings: Greek yogurt, fresh parsley, or a drizzle of olive oil

WHOLE-GRAIN TOAST WITH NUT BUTTER & CHIA

Prep Time : 1 Min

Cook Time : 5 Min

Ingredients:

- 1 slice whole-grain bread
- 1 tbsp almond butter (or peanut butter)
- ½ tsp chia seeds
- ½ banana, sliced

Instructions:

- Toast the whole-grain bread until golden brown.
- Spread almond butter evenly over the toast.
- Sprinkle chia seeds on top.
- Add banana slices for natural sweetness.

Toppings: Greek yogurt, fresh parsley, or a drizzle of olive oil

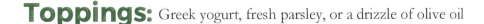

SPAGHETTI SQUASH WITH PESTO CHICKEN

Prep Time : 10 Min

Cook Time : 40 Min

Ingredients:

- 1 medium spaghetti squash, halved and seeds removed
- 1 tbsp olive oil
- 1 chicken breast, grilled and sliced
- 2 tbsp pesto sauce
- ½ tsp salt
- ½ tsp black pepper

Instructions:

- Preheat oven to 400°F (200°C). Brush spaghetti squash halves with olive oil and season with salt and pepper.
- Place cut side down on a baking sheet and roast for 30-35 minutes until tender.
- While squash bakes, grill chicken for 5-7 minutes per side until cooked through. Slice into strips.
- Use a fork to scrape out spaghetti squash strands.
- Toss with pesto sauce and top with sliced grilled chicken.

Toppings: Parmesan cheese, pine nuts, or fresh basil

SWEET POTATO WITH GREEK YOGURT & WALNUTS

Prep Time : 10 Min

Cook Time : 45 Min

Ingredients:

- 1 medium sweet potato
- ½ cup Greek yogurt (unsweetened)
- 2 tbsp walnuts, chopped
- ½ tsp cinnamon

Instructions:

- Preheat oven to 400°F (200°C). Poke holes in the sweet potato with a fork.
- Bake for 40-45 minutes until tender.
- Slice open and fluff the inside with a fork.
- Top with Greek yogurt, walnuts, and cinnamon.

Toppings: Drizzle of honey, pumpkin seeds, or hemp seeds

Chapter 4:
Smart Sugar Hacks – Enjoying Sweets Without the Crash

Who doesn't love a little sweetness? Whether it's a slice of cake, a piece of chocolate, or a spoonful of honey in tea, sugar is deeply embedded in our culture and cravings. But as we know, sugar is also a key driver of glucose spikes, leading to energy crashes, cravings, and long-term health issues.

The good news? You don't have to give up sweets altogether. By using a few smart sugar hacks, you can enjoy your favorite treats without the rollercoaster of spikes and crashes.

Why Sugar Causes Glucose Spikes

When we eat sugar (whether in fruit, desserts, or processed snacks), it is quickly broken down into glucose, entering our bloodstream fast. This creates a sharp spike in blood sugar, triggering the release of insulin to bring levels back down. However, a big insulin response often leads to a crash, leaving us feeling tired, hungry, and craving more sugar. This cycle of spikes and crashes fuels overeating, weight gain, and insulin resistance over time.

Smart Sugar Hacks to Stabilize Glucose Levels

1. Eat Sugar Last

One of the most powerful glucose hacks is simply changing the order in which you eat your food. Eating sweets after a meal containing fiber, protein, and fat significantly reduces the glucose spike.

✅ Hack It: Instead of eating dessert on an empty stomach, have it after a balanced meal to slow sugar absorption.

2. Add Fiber to Your Treats

Fiber slows the absorption of sugar into the bloodstream, preventing rapid spikes. You can enjoy fiber-rich ingredients with a gentler glucose curve by incorporating fiber-rich ingredients into your sweets.

✅ Hack It:

- Use almond flour, coconut flour, or oat flour instead of white flour.
- Add chia seeds, flaxseeds, or psyllium husk to baked goods.
- Include berries, nuts, or shredded coconut for a fiber boost.

3. Pair Sugar with Protein & Fat

When you eat sugar alone, it enters the bloodstream quickly. But when paired with protein and fat, digestion slows, resulting in a smaller glucose response.

✅ Hack It:

- Enjoy dark chocolate with nut butter instead of milk chocolate.
- Pair a banana with Greek yogurt or cottage cheese.
- Add a handful of nuts when snacking on dried fruit.

4. Choose Natural Sweeteners Over Processed Sugar

Not all sugars affect the body in the same way. Refined sugar (like white sugar and high-fructose corn syrup) causes steeper glucose spikes compared to natural alternatives.

✅ Hack It:

- Swap white sugar for raw honey, maple syrup, or coconut sugar (still in moderation!).
- Use stevia or monk fruit as zero-calorie natural alternatives.
- Bake with mashed bananas, applesauce, or dates for natural sweetness.

5. Drink Apple Cider Vinegar Before Sweets

Apple cider vinegar (ACV) contains acetic acid, which slows digestion and reduces glucose spikes when taken before meals.

✅ Hack It:

- Mix 1 tbsp of apple cider vinegar in water and drink 10-15 minutes before eating sweets.
- Add vinegar to salads, dressings, or marinades to naturally regulate glucose.

6. Get Moving After Eating Sweets

A short walk or light exercise after eating helps muscles absorb glucose, preventing it from staying in the bloodstream too long.

✅ Hack It:

- Take a 10-minute walk after meals instead of sitting.
- Do simple bodyweight exercises (squats, lunges, or stretching) for 5 minutes.
- Choose the stairs over the elevator when possible.

7. Choose Dark Chocolate Over Milk Chocolate

Dark chocolate (70% cocoa and above) contains less sugar and more beneficial compounds like antioxidants and fiber, making it a better choice for glucose control.

✅ Hack It:

- Pick chocolate with at least 70% cocoa (the higher, the better).
- Pair dark chocolate with nuts or cheese to slow sugar absorption.
- Melt dark chocolate over berries or nuts for a delicious treat.

8. Make Your Low-Sugar Treats

Homemade desserts let you control the ingredients and reduce added sugars while still satisfying your cravings.

✅ Hack It:

- Replace half the sugar in recipes with mashed bananas or unsweetened applesauce.
- Add protein powder or Greek yogurt to baked goods for balance.
- Use coconut oil, avocado, or nut butter instead of butter or margarine.

Final Thoughts: You Can Still Enjoy Sweets!

The goal isn't to eliminate sugar—it's to be smart about how you consume it. By following these simple sugar hacks, you can enjoy desserts without extreme spikes and crashes, keeping your energy levels stable and your cravings in check🍫🍓✨

SMART SUGAR HACKS

RECIPES

DARK CHOCOLATE ALMOND BITES

Prep Time : 10 Min

Cook Time : 30 Min

Ingredients:

- ½ cup dark chocolate (70% cocoa or higher), melted
- ¼ cup almonds, chopped
- 1 tbsp unsweetened shredded coconut
- 1 tbsp chia seeds
- ½ tsp vanilla extract
- A pinch of sea salt

Instructions:

- Melt the dark chocolate in a microwave or using a double boiler.
- Stir in chopped almonds, shredded coconut, chia seeds, vanilla extract, and sea salt.
- Spoon small portions onto a parchment-lined baking sheet.
- Refrigerate for 30 minutes or until firm.

Toppings: Sprinkle with extra shredded coconut or drizzle with melted nut butter.

CHIA SEED & COCONUT PUDDING

Prep Time : 5 Min

Cook Time : 10 Min

Ingredients:

- ¼ cup chia seeds
- 1 cup unsweetened coconut milk
- ½ tsp vanilla extract
- 1 tbsp monk fruit sweetener (or maple syrup)

Instructions:

- Mix all ingredients in a bowl and stir well.
- Let sit for 5 minutes, then stir again.
- Refrigerate for at least 4 hours (or overnight) until thickened.

Toppings: Fresh berries, shredded coconut, or cinnamon

BERRY & COCONUT YOGURT PARFAIT

Prep Time : 5 Min

Cook Time : 10 Min

Ingredients:

- ½ cup unsweetened Greek yogurt or coconut yogurt
- ½ cup mixed berries (blueberries, strawberries, raspberries)
- 1 tbsp unsweetened shredded coconut
- 1 tbsp chopped nuts (almonds, walnuts, or pecans)
- ½ tsp cinnamon (optional)

Instructions:

- In a glass or bowl, layer Greek yogurt, berries, and shredded coconut.
- Repeat the layers and top with chopped nuts and cinnamon.
- Serve immediately.

Toppings: Add cacao nibs or a drizzle of almond butter for extra flavor.

SUGAR-FREE BANANA MUFFINS

Prep Time : 5 Min

Cook Time : 10 Min

Ingredients:

- 2 ripe bananas, mashed
- 2 cups almond flour
- 2 eggs
- 1 tsp baking powder
- ½ tsp cinnamon
- 1 tbsp coconut oil, melted
- 1 tsp vanilla extract

Instructions:

- Preheat oven to 350°F (175°C) and grease a muffin tin.
- In a bowl, mash the bananas and mix with eggs, coconut oil, and vanilla extract.
- Stir in almond flour, baking powder, and cinnamon until well combined.
- Pour the batter into the muffin tin, filling each cup about ¾ full.
- Bake for 20–25 minutes, or until a toothpick inserted comes out clean.
- Let cool before serving.

Toppings: Sprinkle with chopped nuts or sugar-free dark chocolate chips before baking.

GREEK YOGURT & BERRY PARFAIT

Prep Time : 1 Min

Cook Time : 5 Min

Ingredients:

- ½ cup unsweetened Greek yogurt
- ½ cup mixed berries (strawberries, blueberries, raspberries)
- 1 tbsp chopped nuts (walnuts, almonds)

Instructions:

- Layer Greek yogurt, berries, and nuts in a glass.
- Repeat layers and serve immediately.

Toppings: Chia seeds, a drizzle of honey, or cacao nibs

ALMOND FLOUR BANANA MUFFINS

Prep Time : 5 Min

Cook Time : 30 Min

Ingredients:

- 2 ripe bananas, mashed
- 2 cups almond flour
- 2 eggs
- 1 tsp baking powder
- ½ tsp cinnamon
- 1 tbsp coconut oil

Instructions:

- Preheat oven to 350°F (175°C).
- Mix all ingredients in a bowl until smooth.
- Pour batter into muffin cups and bake for 25 minutes.

Toppings: Chopped nuts or dark chocolate chips

PEANUT BUTTER ENERGY BITES

Prep Time : 5 Min

Cook Time : 30 Min

Ingredients:

- ½ cup natural peanut butter
- ¼ cup ground flaxseeds
- 1 tbsp chia seeds
- 1 tbsp unsweetened cocoa powder
- 1 tsp vanilla extract

Instructions:

- Mix all ingredients in a bowl.
- Roll into small balls and refrigerate for 30 minutes.

Toppings: Shredded coconut or a sprinkle of cinnamon

BAKED APPLES WITH CINNAMON & NUTS

Prep Time : 5 Min

Cook Time : 30 Min

Ingredients:

- 2 apples, cored and halved
- 2 tbsp chopped walnuts
- 1 tsp cinnamon
- 1 tbsp unsweetened coconut oil

Instructions:

- Preheat oven to 375°F (190°C).
- Place apples in a baking dish and sprinkle with walnuts and cinnamon.
- Drizzle with coconut oil and bake for 25 minutes.

Toppings: A dollop of Greek yogurt or a drizzle of almond butter

SUGAR-FREE CHOCOLATE CHIP COOKIES

Prep Time : 5 Min

Cook Time : 20 Min

Ingredients:

- 1 cup almond flour
- ¼ cup sugar-free chocolate chips
- 1 egg
- 1 tbsp coconut oil
- ½ tsp baking soda
- ½ tsp vanilla extract
-

Instructions:

- Preheat oven to 350°F (175°C).
- Mix all ingredients in a bowl until a dough forms.
- Scoop onto a baking sheet and bake for 12 minutes.

Toppings: Dark chocolate drizzle or chopped nuts

COCONUT ALMOND FAT BOMBS

Prep Time : 5 Min

Cook Time : 30 Min

Ingredients:

- ½ cup unsweetened shredded coconut
- ¼ cup almond butter
- 1 tbsp coconut oil
- ½ tsp vanilla extract

Instructions:

- Mix all ingredients in a bowl.
- Form into small balls and freeze for 25 minutes.

Toppings: Crushed almonds or cacao nibs

LOW-SUGAR BAKED OATMEAL CUPS

Prep Time : 5 Min

Cook Time : 25 Min

Ingredients:

- 1 cup rolled oats
- ½ cup mashed banana
- 1 egg
- ½ cup almond milk
- ½ tsp cinnamon

Instructions:

- Preheat oven to 350°F (175°C).
- Mix all ingredients and pour into muffin cups.
- Bake for 20 minutes.

Toppings: Berries, peanut butter, or nuts

FROZEN YOGURT BARK WITH NUTS & BERRIES

Prep Time : 5 Min

Cook Time :

Ingredients:

- 1 cup Greek yogurt
- ¼ cup mixed nuts
- ¼ cup berries

Instructions:

- Spread yogurt onto a parchment-lined baking sheet.
- Sprinkle with nuts and berries.
- Freeze for 3 hours, then break into pieces.

Toppings: Dark chocolate drizzle or coconut flakes

SWEET POTATO BROWNIES

Prep Time : 10 Min

Cook Time : 35 Min

Ingredients:

- 1 cup mashed sweet potato
- ½ cup almond flour
- ¼ cup unsweetened cocoa powder
- 1 egg
- 1 tbsp coconut oil

Instructions:

- Preheat oven to 350°F (175°C).
- Mix all ingredients in a bowl.
- Pour into a baking dish and bake for 30 minutes.

Toppings: Dark chocolate chips or chopped walnuts

KETO CHOCOLATE MOUSSE WITH COCONUT CREAM

Prep Time : 2 Min

Cook Time : 10 Min

Ingredients:

- ½ cup coconut cream
- 2 tbsp unsweetened cocoa powder
- 1 tbsp monk fruit sweetener
- ½ tsp vanilla extract

Instructions:

- Whip all ingredients together until fluffy.
- Chill for 10 minutes before serving.

Toppings: Cacao nibs or shaved dark chocolate

Chapter 5:
Drinks & Their Impact on Blood Sugar

When we think about blood sugar control, we often focus on food—what to eat, when to eat, and how to balance meals. But what we drink can have just as much impact on our glucose levels. The wrong beverages can cause rapid sugar spikes and crashes, leading to energy dips, cravings, and even long-term metabolic issues. The right drinks, on the other hand, can support stable glucose levels, improve hydration, and promote overall health.

How Drinks Affect Blood Sugar

Unlike solid foods, liquids are absorbed much faster because they don't require digestion. This means that sugary drinks can cause almost immediate glucose spikes, overwhelming the body with a surge of sugar. On the flip side, fiber-rich or balanced drinks can help slow glucose absorption and keep energy levels steady.

Let's break down some common beverages and their effects:

The Worst Drinks for Blood Sugar Control

🚫 Soda & Sugary Beverages – These are among the worst offenders. Regular sodas contain 30–50 grams of sugar per serving, causing rapid glucose spikes and insulin surges, leading to energy crashes and cravings.

🚫 Fruit Juices – While fruit itself contains fiber, juices strip away the fiber, leaving behind only the sugar. Even natural juices can spike glucose levels just as fast as soda.

🚫 Energy Drinks – These are often loaded with sugar and caffeine, causing both a glucose spike and an adrenaline rush, followed by a rapid crash.

🚫 Flavored Coffee Drinks – Many coffee shop beverages contain hidden sugars, sometimes more than a can of soda! Even "healthy" alternatives like oat milk lattes can be high in carbs, leading to blood sugar fluctuations.

The Best Drinks for Stable Blood Sugar

✅ Water – The ultimate blood sugar stabilizer. Hydration helps improve insulin sensitivity and prevents dehydration-related sugar cravings. Adding lemon, mint, or cucumber can enhance the flavor naturally.

✅ Herbal Teas – Teas like peppermint, chamomile, ginger, and hibiscus can support digestion, reduce inflammation, and balance blood sugar.

✅ Black Coffee (or with a splash of cream) – Coffee can improve insulin sensitivity and provide a gentle energy boost when consumed without sugar. Avoid artificial creamers and high-carb milk substitutes.

✅ Apple Cider Vinegar Drink – ACV can slow glucose absorption and improve insulin response when consumed before meals. Mix 1 tbsp apple cider vinegar with water and a pinch of cinnamon for a blood sugar-friendly drink.

✅ Fiber-Rich Smoothies – Unlike fruit juices, smoothies with fiber, protein, and fat help stabilize glucose. The key is to avoid high-sugar fruits and include protein, fiber, and healthy fats. (See smoothie recipes in the next section!)

Smart Sugar Hacks for Beverages

✔ If you love soda → Try sparkling water with lime or herbal-infused carbonated drinks.

✔ If you love fruit juice → Blend whole fruits with fiber (like chia seeds) instead of drinking juice alone.

✔ If you need an energy boost → Stick to black coffee or green tea instead of sugar-laden energy drinks.

✔ If you enjoy cocktails → Choose low-sugar mixers like soda water and avoid sugary syrups.

BLOOD SUGAR–FRIENDLY DRINK

RECIPES

APPLE CIDER VINEGAR TONIC

Prep Time : 1 Min
Cook Time : 5 Min

Ingredients:

- 1 tbsp apple cider vinegar
- 1 cup water (still or sparkling)
- ½ tsp cinnamon
- A few drops of stevia (optional)
- 1 tsp lemon juice (optional)

Instructions:

- Mix all ingredients in a glass.
- Stir well and drink before meals for better glucose control.
- If using sparkling water, serve chilled for a refreshing twist.

Benefits: Helps control blood sugar spikes and improves digestion

GREEN SMOOTHIE WITH HEALTHY FATS

Prep Time : 1 Min

Cook Time : 5 Min

Ingredients:

- ½ avocado
- 1 cup unsweetened almond milk
- 1 handful spinach
- 1 tbsp chia seeds or flaxseeds
- ½ tsp cinnamon
- 1 scoop unsweetened protein powder (optional)
- Ice cubes

Instructions:

- Blend all ingredients in a blender until smooth.
- Pour into a glass and enjoy immediately.
- For added flavor, sprinkle with extra cinnamon or shredded coconut

Benefits: Packed with fiber, protein, and healthy fats for stable blood sugar

HERBAL ICED TEA WITH LEMON

Prep Time : 2 Min
Cook Time : 10 Min

Ingredients:

- 1 herbal tea bag (peppermint, chamomile, or hibiscus)
- 1 cup hot water
- 1 tbsp lemon juice
- Ice cubes
- Fresh mint leaves (optional)
- Stevia or monk fruit sweetener (optional)

Instructions:

- Steep the herbal tea bag in hot water for 5–7 minutes.
- Remove the tea bag and let the tea cool slightly.
- Add lemon juice and sweetener if desired.
- Pour over ice and garnish with fresh mint leaves.
- Serve chilled.

Benefits: Hydrating, anti-inflammatory, and caffeine-free

TURMERIC GINGER ANTI-INFLAMMATORY TEA

Prep Time : 2 Min

Cook Time : 10 Min

Ingredients:

- 1 cup hot water
- ½ tsp turmeric powder
- ½ tsp grated ginger
- ¼ tsp cinnamon
- 1 tsp lemon juice
- Stevia or monk fruit sweetener (optional)

Instructions:

- Steep turmeric, ginger, and cinnamon in hot water for 5 minutes.
- Strain, add lemon juice, and sweeten if desired.
- Enjoy warm!

Benefits: Reduces inflammation and supports insulin sensitivity

78

GREEN TEA WITH LEMON

Prep Time : 1 Min

Cook Time : 5 Min

Ingredients:

- 1 green tea bag
- 1 cup hot water
- 1 tsp lemon juice
- A few fresh mint leaves (optional)

Instructions:

- Steep the green tea bag in hot water for 3–5 minutes.
- Add lemon juice and mint leaves for extra flavor.
- Serve hot or chilled.

Benefits: Enhances insulin sensitivity and provides antioxidants

CHIA SEED HYDRATION DRINK

Prep Time : 2 Min

Cook Time : 10 Min

Ingredients:

- 1 tbsp chia seeds
- 1 cup coconut water or plain water
- ½ tsp lime juice
- Stevia (optional)

Instructions:

- Mix chia seeds in water and let sit for 10 minutes until gel-like.
- Add lime juice and stevia if desired.
- Stir and drink chilled.

Benefits: Supports hydration and slows glucose absorption

CINNAMON-SPICED HOT COCOA

Prep Time : 1 Min
Cook Time : 5 Min

Ingredients:

- 1 cup unsweetened almond or coconut milk
- 1 tbsp unsweetened cacao powder
- ½ tsp cinnamon
- ½ tsp vanilla extract
- Stevia or monk fruit sweetener (optional)

Instructions:

- Warm almond milk over low heat.
- Whisk in cacao powder, cinnamon, and vanilla.
- Sweeten to taste and serve warm.

Benefits: A blood sugar-friendly chocolate fix.

BERRY PROTEIN SMOOTHIE

Prep Time : 1 Min

Cook Time : 5 Min

Ingredients:

- ½ cup frozen mixed berries
- 1 cup unsweetened almond milk
- 1 scoop protein powder (unsweetened)
- 1 tbsp chia seeds
- Ice cubes

Instructions:

- Blend all ingredients until smooth.
- Serve immediately.

Benefits: High-fiber, high-protein, and low in sugar

SUGAR-FREE ICED MATCHA LATTE

Prep Time : 1 Min
Cook Time : 5 Min

Ingredients:

- 1 tsp matcha powder
- 1 cup unsweetened almond or coconut milk
- ½ tsp vanilla extract
- Ice cubes
- Stevia (optional)

Instructions:

- Whisk matcha powder with a splash of hot water.
- Add almond milk, ice cubes, and sweetener.
- Stir well and serve cold.

Benefits: Provides antioxidants and steady energy

LEMON GINGER SPARKLING WATER

Prep Time : 1 Min

Cook Time : 5 Min

Ingredients:

- 1 cup sparkling water
- 1 tsp fresh grated ginger
- 1 tbsp lemon juice
- Ice cubes

Instructions:

- Mix all ingredients in a glass.
- Let the ginger infuse for 5 minutes, then enjoy!

Benefits: Refreshing, gut-friendly, and helps reduce bloating

VANILLA ALMOND CHAI LATTE

Prep Time : 1 Min
Cook Time : 5 Min

Ingredients:

- 1 chai tea bag
- 1 cup unsweetened almond milk
- ½ tsp vanilla extract
- ½ tsp cinnamon
- Stevia (optional)

Instructions:

- Steep chai tea bag in hot almond milk for 5 minutes.
- Add vanilla, cinnamon, and sweetener if desired.
- Stir and serve warm.

Benefits: A cozy drink without the sugar rush

SPARKLING CITRUS MINT MOCKTAIL

Prep Time : 1 Min

Cook Time : 5 Min

Ingredients:

- 1 cup sparkling water
- 1 tbsp fresh lime juice
- 1 tbsp fresh orange juice (or lemon juice for a lower-carb option)
- Fresh mint leaves
- Ice cubes

Instructions:

- Muddle mint leaves at the bottom of a glass.
- Add lime juice, orange juice, and ice cubes.
- Top with sparkling water and stir gently.
- Topping idea: Garnish with an orange or lemon slice.

Benefits: A refreshing, sugar-free alternative to traditional cocktails

CREAMY COCONUT BERRY SMOOTHIE

Prep Time : 1 Min
Cook Time : 5 Min

Ingredients:

- ½ cup frozen mixed berries
- ¾ cup unsweetened coconut milk
- 1 tbsp chia seeds
- ½ tsp cinnamon
- 1 scoop unsweetened protein powder (optional)
- Ice cubes

Instructions:

- Blend all ingredients until smooth.
- Pour into a glass and enjoy immediately.
- Topping idea: Sprinkle with unsweetened shredded coconut or crushed walnuts.

Benefits: High in fiber and healthy fats to slow glucose absorption

AVOCADO CACAO SMOOTHIE

Prep Time : 1 Min

Cook Time : 5 Min

Ingredients:

- ½ avocado
- 1 cup unsweetened almond milk
- 1 tbsp unsweetened cacao powder
- ½ tsp cinnamon
- ½ tsp vanilla extract
- A few drops of stevia (optional)
- Ice cubes

Instructions:

- Blend all ingredients until creamy and smooth.
- Pour into a glass and enjoy chilled.
- Topping idea: Sprinkle with cacao nibs or a pinch of sea salt.

Benefits: Loaded with healthy fats, fiber, and antioxidants for steady energy

BERRY BASIL MOCKTAIL

Prep Time : 1 Min
Cook Time : 5 Min

Ingredients:

- ½ cup fresh or frozen berries (strawberries, raspberries, or blueberries)
- 1 cup sparkling water
- 1 tbsp fresh lemon juice
- Fresh basil leaves
- Ice cubes

Instructions:

- Muddle berries and basil leaves in a glass.
- Add lemon juice and ice cubes.
- Pour in sparkling water and stir well.
- Topping idea: Garnish with extra basil or a few whole berries.

Benefits: Packed with antioxidants and refreshing flavors

Chapter 6:
Blood Sugar-Friendly Snacks & Meal Prep

In our fast-paced lives, snacking is inevitable, but the key is choosing options that stabilize blood sugar rather than cause energy crashes. The right snacks should include fiber, healthy fats, and protein to slow glucose absorption and keep cravings at bay.

This chapter will help you master quick, portable snack ideas and smart meal prep strategies to make blood sugar-friendly eating effortless.

Quick, Portable Snacks for Balanced Blood Sugar

When hunger strikes, reach for nutrient-dense, low-glycemic snacks that will keep you fueled without causing a sugar crash. Here are some easy grab-and-go ideas:

✅ **Protein & Fat-Based Snacks:**
- Nut butter with celery or cucumber slices
- Hard-boiled eggs with sea salt and paprika
- Greek yogurt with chia seeds and cinnamon
- **Cheese slices with almonds or walnuts**

✅ **Fiber-Packed Snacks:**
- Avocado with hemp seeds and lime
- Hummus with raw veggies (carrots, bell peppers, cucumbers)
- Chia pudding with unsweetened coconut and berries
- Flaxseed crackers with guacamole

✅ **Low-Glycemic Sweet Options:**
- Berries with cottage cheese or nut butter
- Dark chocolate (85% cacao or higher) with almonds
- Coconut yogurt with cinnamon and walnuts
- Sugar-free protein bars (homemade or low-carb options)

Meal Prep Strategies for Blood Sugar Balance

Planning ahead ensures you always have healthy options available, reducing the temptation for blood sugar-spiking foods. Here's how:

✔ Batch Cooking: Prepare proteins (chicken, turkey, tofu, boiled eggs) and fiber-rich veggies (roasted Brussels sprouts, kale, bell peppers) in advance.

✔ Pre-Portion Snacks: Store nut mixes, hummus, or Greek yogurt in individual containers for grab-and-go convenience.

✔ Smart Storage: Keep low-glycemic fruits (berries, avocado) and protein sources (boiled eggs, cheese, yogurt) easily accessible in your fridge.

✔ Freezer-Friendly Prep: Make smoothie packs, soups, and fiber-packed muffins to store in the freezer for quick meals.

BLOOD SUGAR–FRIENDLY SNACKS

RECIPE

HARD-BOILED EGG & HUMMUS PLATE

Prep Time : 1 Min

Cook Time : 5 Min

Ingredients:

- 2 hard-boiled eggs, sliced
- 3 tbsp hummus (store-bought or homemade)
- 1 tsp olive oil
- 1 tbsp pumpkin seeds
- ½ tsp paprika
- Cucumber and carrot sticks for dipping

Instructions:

- Slice the hard-boiled eggs and arrange them on a plate.
- Drizzle hummus with olive oil and sprinkle with paprika.
- Add pumpkin seeds on top for extra crunch.
- Serve with cucumber and carrot sticks.

Toppings: Sprinkle with hemp seeds or chili flakes for extra flavor.

Benefits: High in protein and healthy fats for steady energy

SPICED NUTS & SEEDS MIX

Prep Time : 1 Min

Cook Time : 5 Min

Ingredients:

- ½ cup almonds
- ½ cup walnuts
- ¼ cup pumpkin seeds
- ¼ cup sunflower seeds
- ½ tsp cinnamon
- ¼ tsp cayenne pepper (optional)
- ½ tsp sea salt
- 1 tbsp coconut oil (melted)

Instructions:

- Toss all nuts and seeds in a bowl with coconut oil, cinnamon, and cayenne pepper.
- Spread onto a baking sheet and toast in the oven at 300°F (150°C) for 5–7 minutes.
- Let cool and store in an airtight container for quick snacking.

Toppings: Sprinkle with unsweetened coconut flakes or dark chocolate chips for variety.

Benefits: A portable, protein-rich snack with fiber and healthy fats

COTTAGE CHEESE & BERRIES BOWL

Prep Time : 1 Min

Cook Time : 3 Min

Ingredients:

- ½ cup full-fat cottage cheese
- ¼ cup mixed berries (blueberries, raspberries, or strawberries)
- 1 tbsp chia seeds
- ½ tsp cinnamon
- 1 tbsp chopped walnuts

Instructions:

- Scoop cottage cheese into a bowl.
- Top with fresh berries, chia seeds, and cinnamon.
- Sprinkle with walnuts for added crunch.

Toppings: Add a drizzle of almond butter for extra richness.

Benefits: High in protein, low in sugar, and packed with fiber

GREEK YOGURT & FLAXSEED POWER BOWL

Prep Time : 1 Min

Cook Time : 3 Min

Ingredients:

- ¾ cup full-fat Greek yogurt
- 1 tbsp ground flaxseeds
- ¼ cup mixed berries
- ½ tsp cinnamon

Instructions:

- Combine all ingredients in a bowl.
- Stir well and enjoy immediately or store in a container for later.

Benefits: High in protein, omega-3s, and gut-friendly probiotics

ALMOND BUTTER & CHIA SEED ENERGY BITES

Prep Time : 2 Min

Cook Time : 10 Min

Ingredients:

- ½ cup almond butter
- ½ cup ground flaxseeds
- ¼ cup chia seeds
- 1 tsp cinnamon
- 1 tbsp unsweetened shredded coconut
- 1 tsp vanilla extract

Instructions:

- Mix all ingredients in a bowl.
- Roll into small balls and refrigerate for at least 30 minutes before eating.

Benefits: Portable, protein-packed snack to fight cravings

GUACAMOLE & FLAXSEED CRACKERS

Prep Time : 1 Min

Cook Time : 5 Min

Ingredients:

- 1 ripe avocado
- ½ lime (juiced)
- ½ tsp sea salt
- ¼ tsp black pepper
- ¼ cup flaxseed crackers

Instructions:

- Mash avocado with lime juice, salt, and pepper.
- Serve with flaxseed crackers for dipping.

Benefits: Healthy fats and fiber for steady blood sugar

TURKEY & AVOCADO LETTUCE WRAPS

Prep Time : 1 Min

Cook Time : 5 Min

Ingredients:

- 3 slices turkey breast
- ½ avocado, sliced
- 3 large lettuce leaves
- ½ tsp Dijon mustard

Instructions:

- Spread mustard on turkey slices.
- Place avocado slices on top.
- Wrap in lettuce leaves and roll tightly.

Benefits: Low-carb, high-protein snack

ROASTED CHICKPEAS WITH PAPRIKA

Prep Time : 5 Min

Cook Time : 30 Min

Ingredients:

- 1 can chickpeas (drained and rinsed)
- 1 tbsp olive oil
- 1 tsp paprika
- ½ tsp sea salt

Instructions:

- Toss chickpeas with oil, paprika, and salt.
- Roast at 375°F (190°C) for 25–30 minutes, shaking the pan halfway through.

Benefits: High in fiber and plant-based protein

CHEESE & WALNUT SNACK BOX

Prep Time : 5 Min

Cook Time : 30 Min

Ingredients:

- 2 oz cheese (cheddar, gouda, or mozzarella)
- ¼ cup walnuts
- 5 cucumber slices

Instructions:

- Slice cheese into cubes.
- Arrange cheese, walnuts, and cucumber slices in a container.

Benefits: Quick grab-and-go protein and fat source

HARD-BOILED EGG & AVOCADO BOWL

Prep Time : 2 Min

Cook Time : 10 Min

Ingredients:

- 2 hard-boiled eggs, sliced
- ½ avocado, diced
- ½ tsp olive oil
- ¼ tsp sea salt
- Black pepper to taste

Instructions:

- Toss all ingredients together in a bowl.

Benefits: Packed with protein and healthy fats

CAULIFLOWER HUMMUS & VEGGIES

Prep Time : 5 Min

Cook Time : 15 Min

Ingredients:

- 1 cup steamed cauliflower
- 2 tbsp tahini
- 1 clove garlic
- 1 tbsp lemon juice
- ½ tsp cumin
- ¼ tsp sea salt

Instructions:

- Blend all ingredients until smooth.
- Serve with cucumber, celery, and carrot sticks.

Benefits: Low-carb, high-fiber dip alternative

SMOKED SALMON & AVOCADO ROLL-UPS

Prep Time : 1 Min

Cook Time : 5 Min

Ingredients:

- 3 slices smoked salmon
- ½ avocado, sliced
- 1 tsp lemon juice
- ½ tsp black pepper

Instructions:

- Layer avocado slices onto smoked salmon.
- Roll up and secure with a toothpick.

Benefits: Rich in omega-3s and protein

COTTAGE CHEESE & SUNFLOWER SEED MIX

Prep Time : 1 Min

Cook Time : 3 Min

Ingredients:

- ½ cup full-fat cottage cheese
- 1 tbsp sunflower seeds
- ½ tsp cinnamon

Instructions:

- Mix all ingredients together.

Benefits: High-protein, nutrient-dense snack

ALMOND BUTTER & APPLE SLICES

Prep Time : 1 Min

Cook Time : 3 Min

Ingredients:

- 1 apple, sliced
- 1 tbsp almond butter

Instructions:

- Spread almond butter on apple slices.

Benefits: A balanced mix of fiber, protein, and healthy fats

PUMPKIN SEED & COCONUT ENERGY BARS

Prep Time : 5 Min

Cook Time : 20 Min

Ingredients:

- ½ cup pumpkin seeds
- ¼ cup unsweetened coconut flakes
- 1 tbsp chia seeds
- 2 tbsp almond butter
- 1 tsp cinnamon
- 1 tbsp coconut oil

Instructions:

- Mix all ingredients and press into a small baking dish.
- Refrigerate for 1 hour, then cut into bars.

Benefits: A sugar-free alternative to granola bars

Bonus

Weekly Snack Plan

Monday: Hard-Boiled Egg & Hummus Plate + Roasted Chickpeas

Tuesday: Cottage Cheese & Berries Bowl + Cheese & Walnut Box

Wednesday: Almond Butter & Apple Slices + Turkey & Avocado Wraps

Thursday: Greek Yogurt & Flaxseed Bowl + Spiced Nuts & Seeds Mix

Friday: Cauliflower Hummus & Veggies + Pumpkin Seed Energy Bars

Saturday: Guacamole & Flaxseed Crackers + Smoked Salmon Roll-Ups

Sunday: Spiced Nuts & Seeds Mix + Cottage Cheese & Sunflower Seed Mix

Made in United States
Troutdale, OR
05/01/2025

31017021R00062